HMH | into Reading™

myBook 1

my Book 1

Authors and Advisors

Alma Flor Ada • Kylene Beers • F. Isabel Campoy

Joyce Armstrong Carroll • Nathan Clemens

Anne Cunningham • Martha C. Hougen

Elena Izquierdo • Carol Jago • Erik Palmer

Robert E. Probst • Shane Templeton • Julie Washington

Contributing Consultants

David Dockterman • Mindset Works®

Jill Eggleton

Printed in the U.S.A.

ISBN   978-0-544-45879-6

10   0868   27 26 25 24 23 22

4500845437   C D E F G

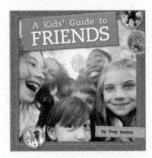

5

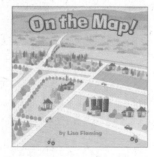

Nice to Meet You!

"Make new friends and keep the old.
One is silver and the other gold."

—Traditional Song

? Essential Question

How can making new friends and learning new things help us?

Get Curious Video

Words About New Friends and Experiences

Complete the Vocabulary Network to show what you know about the words.

friendship

Meaning: When you have a **friendship** with someone, you like the person.

Synonyms and Antonyms	Drawing

emotions

Meaning: **Emotions** are strong feelings we have, like happiness or sadness.

Synonyms and Antonyms	Drawing

challenge

Meaning: A **challenge** is something that is hard to do.

Synonyms and Antonyms	Drawing

My First Day

my writing ideas

It was my first day of school!
There was so much to do!

First, we sang.

Next, we listened to a story.
I did all my work.

Then, we played.
It was fun!

Last, we said goodbye.
See you tomorrow!

Prepare to Read

GENRE STUDY ▸ **Narrative nonfiction** gives information, but it sounds like a story. Look for:

- photos that show real people
- photos that show real places
- facts about a real topic

SET A PURPOSE ▸ **Ask questions** before, during, and after you read to help you get information or understand the text. Look for evidence in the text and pictures to **answer** the questions.

POWER WORDS
new
try
great
enjoy
excited
nervous

Meet Pam Muñoz Ryan.

Try This!

by Pam Muñoz Ryan

We go to school.

This is new.
Try this, Sam!

We like this bus.

This bus is great!

We go to new rooms.

This is new.
Try to paint, Sam!

We go outside at school.

This is new.
Try to bat, Sam!

School is great!
We like to try.

Turn and Talk

Use details from **Try This!** to answer these questions with a partner.

1. **Ask and Answer Questions** What questions did you ask yourself about **Try This!** before, during, and after reading? How did your questions help you understand the text?

2. How does Sam feel at the end? Tell why.

Listening Tip

Listen carefully. Look at your partner to show that you are paying attention.

Write a Caption

PROMPT Look back at **Try This!** What new things does Sam try to do?

PLAN First, draw a picture of something new Sam does.

Try This!

WRITE Now write a sentence to be a caption for your picture. Tell about the new thing Sam does. Use this for help:

Sam can _____.

Remember to:

• Begin with a capital letter.

• End with a period.

Prepare to Read

GENRE STUDY **Narrative nonfiction** gives information, but it sounds like a story.

MAKE A PREDICTION Preview **We Try, We Paint**. Children go to a new room at school. What do you think they will do there?

_____

- -

_____

- -

_____

- -

_____

SET A PURPOSE Ask yourself questions before, during, and after reading to help you get information about what the children do.

We Try, We Paint

READ What do the children do in the new room? <u>Underline</u> it.

We see a new room at school.

We go to this room to paint.

Try to paint!

We paint the bus.

We like this bus.

This bus is great! ▶

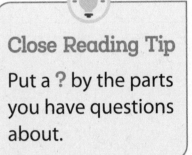

Close Reading Tip

Put a **?** by the parts you have questions about.

CHECK MY UNDERSTANDING

Write a question you have about this text.

_____

_____

_____

_____

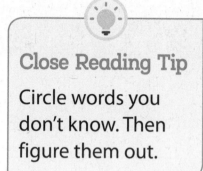

READ What do the children paint now? <u>Underline</u> it.

We paint the school.

We like this school.

This school is great!

We try.

We paint!

This new room is great!

We like to paint at school.

Close Reading Tip

Circle words you don't know. Then figure them out.

CHECK MY UNDERSTANDING

Why did the author write this text? What does the author want you to learn from it?

_____

- -

_____

- -

_____

- -

_____

DRAW IT Think about what the children paint in the room. Draw a picture of the thing you like best. Add your own details. Write a label for the picture.

_____

- -

_____

Prepare to Read

GENRE STUDY **Realistic fiction** stories are made up but could happen in real life. Look for:

- characters who are like real people
- places that seem real
- events that could really happen

SET A PURPOSE As you read, stop and think if you don't understand something. Reread, look at the pictures, use what you already know, or ask yourself questions.

Meet Elisa Chavarri.

My School Trip

by Aly G. Mays

illustrated by Elisa Chavarri

We took a school trip.

First, we took a bus.
Nan was my partner.

Nan was new at school.
Was Nan mad?
Was Nan sad?

The trip was to Butterfly Garden!

Pam had a butterfly.
Dan had a butterfly.

I wished I had a butterfly.

I had a butterfly!
Nan was sad.

Nan had a butterfly!
Nan was happy at last.

Nan is my new friend.
My school trip was great!

Turn and Talk

Use details from **My School Trip** to answer these questions with a partner.

1. **Monitor and Clarify** When you came to a part you did not understand, what did you do to try to figure it out?

2. How can you tell that the two girls become friends?

Talking Tip

Ask a question if you are not sure about your partner's ideas.

Why did you say _____?

Write a List

PROMPT Look back at **My School Trip**. What does the girl who is telling the story like about her trip?

PLAN First, draw or write four things the girl likes about her trip.

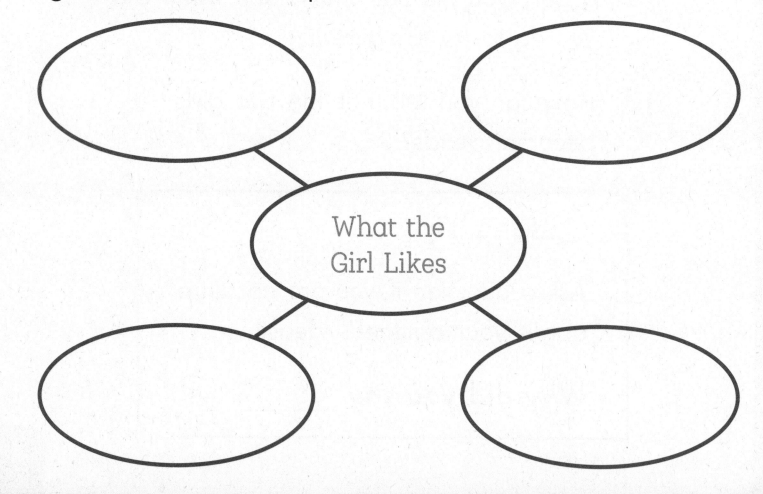

What the
Girl Likes

WRITE Now write a list of things that the girl telling the story likes about her trip. Remember to:

- List people, places, or things the girl likes.
- Use the words and pictures from the story and your web for ideas.

Prepare to Read

GENRE STUDY **Realistic fiction** stories are made up but could happen in real life.

MAKE A PREDICTION Preview **A Trip to a Garden**. A girl and her dad take a trip to a garden. What do you think they will see there?

_____

- -

_____

- -

_____

- -

_____

SET A PURPOSE Read to find out what happens at the garden.

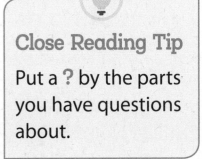

A Trip to a Garden

READ Where do the girl and her dad go on a trip? <u>Underline</u> it.

I am Nan.

This is my dad.

We like to go outside.

We go to see a garden.

This is my first trip to the garden.

We see a tan cat at the garden.

The cat likes my dad! ▶

Close Reading Tip

Put a **?** by the parts you have questions about.

CHECK MY UNDERSTANDING

What do Nan and her dad see at the garden?
Go back and read again if you are not sure.

_____

- -

_____

READ What else do the girl and her dad see? <u>Underline</u> it. If you don't know, look at the picture for help. What else can you do to help yourself understand?

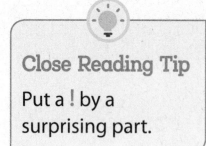

Close Reading Tip

Put a ! by a surprising part.

I see a butterfly at the garden.

Can my dad see the butterfly?

He can see the butterfly!

My dad is happy.

We see a new butterfly.

We like this new butterfly.

I am happy.

This is a great trip!

CHECK MY UNDERSTANDING

Why do you think the author wrote this story?

_____

_ _

_____

_ _

_____

_ _

_____

DRAW IT Draw a picture of what Nan and her dad like about going to the garden. Write a sentence to tell about your picture.

Prepare to Read

GENRE STUDY **Informational text** is nonfiction. It gives facts about a topic. Look for:

- facts about friends
- headings that stand out
- photos with labels

SET A PURPOSE Read to make smart guesses, or **inferences**, about things the author does not say. Use what you already know and clues in the text and pictures to help you.

POWER WORDS
kinds
together

Build Background: Kinds of Friends

A Kids' Guide to
FRIENDS

by Trey Amico

Kinds of Friends

A friend is nice.

A friend likes to be with you.

A friend makes you happy.

Who can be your friend?

classmate

neighbor

Grandma

Dad

sister

cat

There are all kinds of friends!

Fun with Friends

Friends play.
Friends can be silly.
Friends like to be together.
What else can friends do?

run

dig

ride

read

jump

laugh

The best times are with friends!

Make New Friends

School is one place to find friends.
Look around.

Be brave.

Say hi.

Ask someone to play with you.

Be fair.

Take turns.

Say sorry if you make a mistake.

Cheer each other up.

What else do good friends do?

smile

wave

listen

share

help

play

Try to make your friends happy!

It feels good to be a friend.
Let's be friends!

Use details from **A Kids' Guide to Friends** to answer these questions with a partner.

1. Make Inferences Why is it a good idea to make new friends?

2. What are some different ways to be a good friend?

Talking Tip

Wait for your turn to speak. Tell about your ideas and feelings clearly.

I feel that _____.

Write an Opinion

PROMPT Think about the different ways to make friends in **A Kids' Guide to Friends**. Which way do you think is the best?

PLAN First, draw a picture. Show you making a new friend, using the best way you learned from **A Kids' Guide to Friends**.

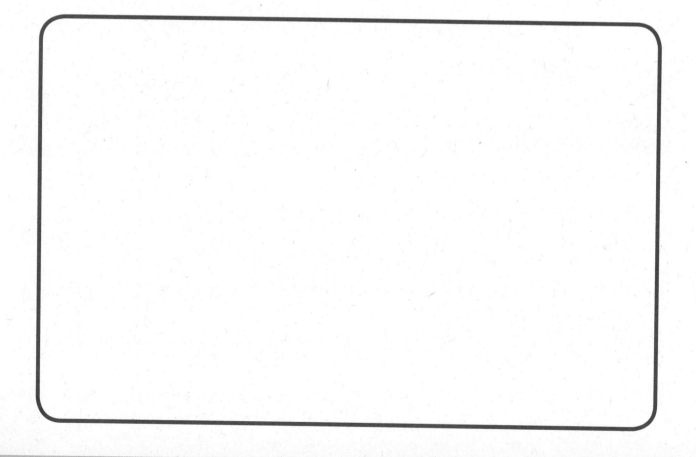

WRITE Now write a sentence to tell which way of making friends you think is the best. Then write a reason why you think it is best. Remember to:

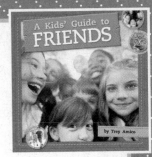

- Tell your opinion.

- Use the word **because** when you write your reason.

Prepare to Read

GENRE STUDY **Informational text** is nonfiction. It gives facts about a topic.

MAKE A PREDICTION Preview **Good Friends**. You know that informational text has facts. What do you think you will learn from this text?

_____

- -

_____

_____

- -

_____

_____

_____

- -

_____

SET A PURPOSE Read to find out some of the things good friends do.

Good Friends

READ Think about what the text is mainly about.

Good friends like to go to school together.
Friends like to go outside.
A friend is sad.
A good friend is sorry.
A friend is mad.
A good friend is fair. ▶

Close Reading Tip

Mark important ideas with *.

CHECK MY UNDERSTANDING

How can you help a friend who is sad or mad?

READ How can you help a new classmate? <u>Underline</u> it.

A classmate is new at school.

At first, the classmate is sad.

A good friend is brave.

Go to the new classmate.

This is a new friend.

The new friend is happy!

New friends enjoy school together.

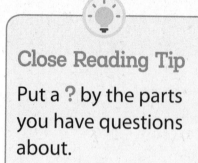

Close Reading Tip

Put a **?** by the parts you have questions about.

CHECK MY UNDERSTANDING

What is the main thing, or central idea, the text is about?

WRITE ABOUT IT Think about how the good friends act in **Good Friends**. Why do you think the new friend is happy?

_____

- -

_____

_____

- -

_____

_____

- -

_____

_____

- -

_____

_____

- -

_____

_____

- -

_____

_____

- -

_____

Prepare to Read

GENRE STUDY **Fairy tales** are old stories that have made-up characters and events that could not happen. Look for:

- phrases like **Once upon a time**
- a happy ending

SET A PURPOSE **Ask questions** before, during, and after you read to help you understand the text and get information. Look for evidence in the text and pictures to **answer** your questions.

POWER WORDS

ugly

paddled

chilly

beautiful

changed

Meet Gail Carson Levine.

Big Dilly's Tale

by Gail Carson Levine
illustrated by Jui Ishida

Once upon a time, Dilly was a
BIG duckling with a BIG beak.
A duck called him ugly.

His friend Minna called him cute.
Dilly splashed. Splat!

One day, Dilly paddled fast for fun.
But when he turned, he was alone.
And lost.
And afraid.

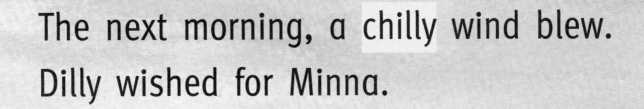

The next morning, a chilly wind blew.
Dilly wished for Minna.

Then Dilly saw a girl.
She led him to her farm.

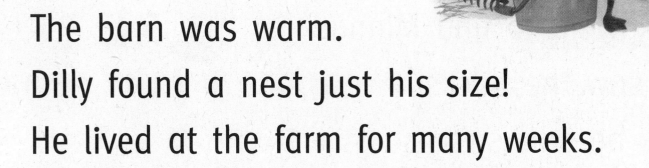

The barn was warm.

Dilly found a nest just his size!

He lived at the farm for many weeks.

When spring came,
Dilly went to find Minna.
He saw the ducks!
And he saw swans.

Dilly looked at himself.

Oh! He saw a swan!

Dilly was not a duck after all!

Minna said he was still cute.

Dilly played with the swans and
Minna and the other ducks.
He lived happily ever after!

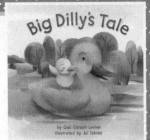

Big Dilly's Tale

by Gail Carson Levine
Illustrated by Jui Ishida

Use details from **Big Dilly's Tale** to answer these questions with a partner.

1. **Ask and Answer Questions** What questions did you ask yourself about Dilly before, during, and after reading? How did they help you understand the story?

2. What does Dilly learn about himself?

Talking Tip

Complete the sentence to add to what your partner says.

My idea is _____.

Write a Description

PROMPT What is Dilly like in **Big Dilly's Tale**? Use ideas from the words and pictures in the story to help you describe Dilly.

PLAN First, write words to tell what Dilly looks like. Tell how he sounds and acts.

Looks	Sounds	Acts

WRITE Now write sentences to describe what Dilly is like and why he does the things he does. Remember to:

- Use words that tell how Dilly looks, sounds, and acts. Tell why he acts that way.

- Put a period at the end of each sentence.

_____

- -

_____

_____

- -

_____

- -

_____

- -

_____

- -

_____

Prepare to Read

GENRE STUDY **Fairy tales** are old stories that have made-up characters and events that could not happen.

MAKE A PREDICTION Preview **The Map**. A brave duck wants to find new friends. Where do you think the duck will look for them?

_____

- -

_____

- -

_____

SET A PURPOSE Ask yourself questions about **The Map** before, during, and after reading to help you find out what Duck does and to understand the story.

The Map

READ How does Duck get to the farm? <u>Underline</u> words that tell.

Brave Duck took a trip to find new friends.

She had a map.

Tap, tap, tap, on the map!

The map took Duck to a farm.

Sad Cat was at the farm.

Sad Cat was happy to see Duck.

Duck had a new friend! ▶

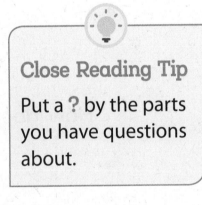

Close Reading Tip

Put a **?** by the parts you have questions about.

CHECK MY UNDERSTANDING

Write a question you have about the story.

_____

_____

_____

_____

_____

READ Duck and Cat use the amazing map. Where do they go? Who do they meet? <u>Underline</u> words that tell.

Close Reading Tip

Write C when you make a connection.

Duck and Cat wished to find a new friend.

Tap, tap, tap, on the map!

The map took Duck and Cat to a garden.

Sad Butterfly was in the garden.

Sad Butterfly was happy to see Duck and Cat.

Duck had new friends at last!

Then the new friends had fun together.

CHECK MY UNDERSTANDING

How does Duck feel at the end of the story? Why?

_____

_____

_____

_____

_____

_____

_____

WRITE ABOUT IT What do Duck, Cat, and Butterfly do now? Add to the story. Draw a picture on another sheet of paper to go with your writing.

Prepare to View

GENRE STUDY **Songs** are words set to music.
We can sing them out loud. Listen for:

- the tune, or how the song sounds
- words that repeat
- how the song makes you feel

SET A PURPOSE Watch to find out who the
characters are and what they look like.
Find out what the characters do and say.
This will help you understand how they
feel and why they act the way they do.

Meet The FuZees.

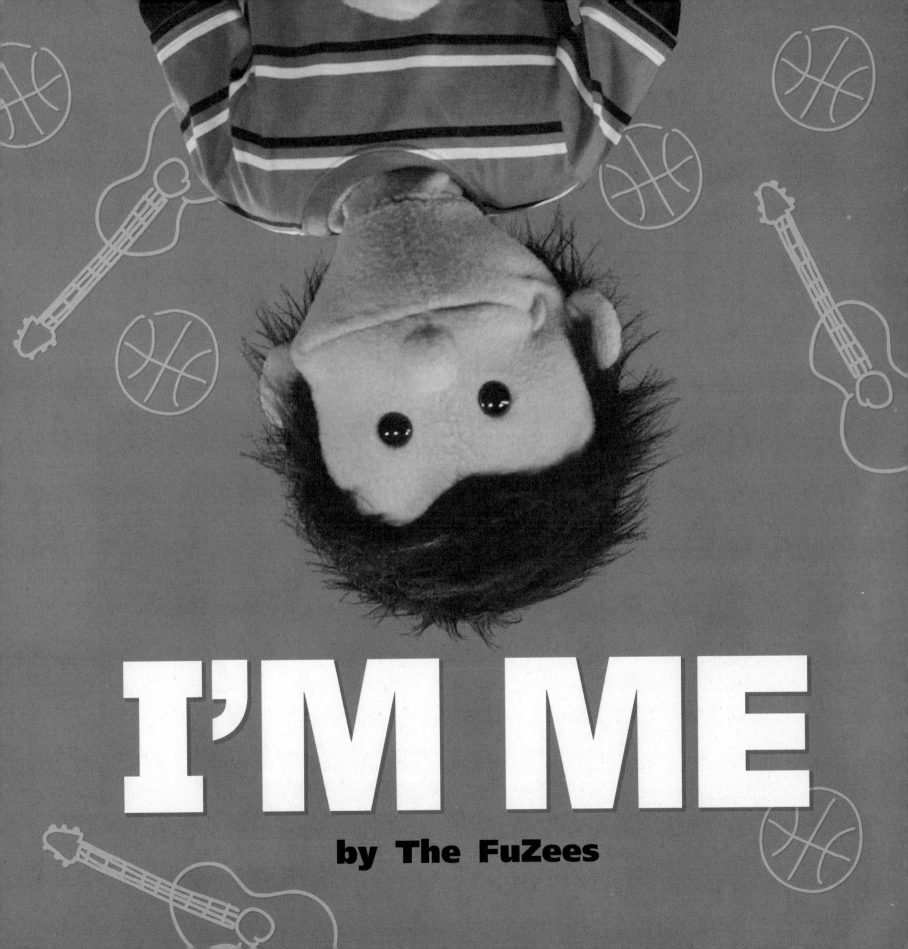

I'M ME

by The FuZees

As You View Get to know the characters! Think about the words of the song. Watch for the pictures that pop up. Use details in the pictures and the song to help you understand what the characters like, what makes them special, and why they act the way they do.

I'M ME
by The FuZees

Use details from **I'm Me** to answer these questions with a partner.

1. **Characters** Describe what the characters are like. What things do they like? Why do the characters do the things they do?

2. Why do the characters think it is good to be unique?

Listening Tip

Listen carefully and politely. Look at your partner to show that you are paying attention.

Let's Wrap Up!

 **Essential Question**

How can making new friends and learning new things help us?

Pick one of these activities to show what you have learned about the topic.

1. **Welcome to Our Class!**

How could you help a new student feel welcome in your class? Make a poster with words and pictures. Use ideas from the texts you have read about friends.

2. Cheer for Friends!

Think about something new you and a friend tried to do or want to try to do. Make up a cheer that describes it. Practice the cheer. Then share it with the class.

Word Challenge
Try to use the word friendship in your cheer.

My Notes

My Family, My Community

"Your heart will lead you home!"
—Hispanic Proverb

? Essential Question

How does everyone in my family and community make them special?

Get Curious Video

Words About Communities

Complete the Vocabulary Network to show what you know about the words.

area
Meaning: An **area** is a part of a bigger place.

Synonyms and Antonyms	Drawing

population

Meaning: The **population** is the number of people who live in a place.

Synonyms and Antonyms	Drawing

working

Meaning: If you are **working**, you are doing a job.

Synonyms and Antonyms	Drawing

Kids Speak Up!

Why is the place where you live great?

I think my town is great!
It has a big park.
We can play ball.

LIBRARY

I like my town
because it has
a library. I get
tons of books!

The workers make my
town great. Firefighters
put out fires FAST!

I love my town!
It has a lake.
My dad and
I go fishing.

97

Prepare to Read

GENRE STUDY **Realistic fiction** stories are made up but could happen in real life. Look for:

- characters who have problems that real people might have
- places that seem real

SET A PURPOSE Read to understand events in the beginning, middle, and end. Look for details in the words and pictures to help you. **Retell** the events in your own words.

POWER WORDS

mess

market

sell

help

neighbors

set

Meet Wong Herbert Yee.

Dan Had a Plan

by Wong Herbert Yee

"Hi, Dan," said Kim.

"Can you see my bugs and bats?"

"I see a big mess!" said Dan.

"We will go to the farmers' market.
We will sell the bugs and bats.
The money is for new library books."

"I like bugs and bats," said Dan.
"I like books. Can I help?"
"You are too little," said Kim.

Dad and the neighbors set up.
"Hi, kids!" said Dad.

"Hi, Sam," said Dan.

"Hi," said Sam. "Can I buy a bat?"

"Did you see the big sign?" asked Dan.

Dan had a plan.

"We can help!" said Dan.

"BUY A BUG!" said Dan.
"BUY A BAT!" said Sam.

"Is it good?" asked Tim.
"It is GREAT!" said Sam.
Tim ran to buy a bat.

"Can I buy a bug?" asked Pam.
"You can!" said Dan.

Many neighbors had bugs and bats.

Kim had the last one!
Dan was sad.

"You are little," said Kim.
"You are a big help, too!"

The new books are at the library.
"We did it!" said Dan and Sam.

Use details from **Dan Had a Plan** to answer these questions with a partner.

1. **Retell** Tell the story in your own words. Tell the main things that happen first, next, and last.

2. How does Kim feel about Dan at the end of the story? Why?

Listening Tip

Look at your partner. Show that you are interested in what your partner says.

Write a Plan

PROMPT Look back at **Dan Had a Plan**. What steps do Dan and Sam follow to sell the fruit snacks?

PLAN First, write or draw what Dan and Sam do first, next, and last in their plan.

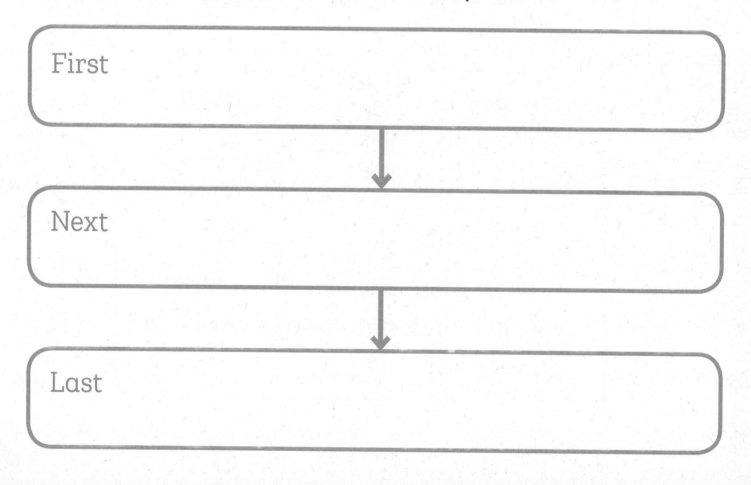

First

Next

Last

WRITE Now write sentences to explain what Dan and Sam do to sell the fruit snacks. Remember to:

- Use the words **first**, **next**, and **last**.

- Begin each sentence with a capital letter. End it with a period.

Prepare to Read

GENRE STUDY **Realistic fiction** stories are made up but could happen in real life.

MAKE A PREDICTION Preview **Together**. Three friends like to help their neighbors. What do you think they will do?

_____

- -

_____

_____

- -

_____

_____

- -

_____

SET A PURPOSE Read to find out how the friends help their neighbors. Find out if your prediction is right.

Together

READ How do the kids help? <u>Underline</u> words that tell.

Kim, Pam, and Sam are friends.

The kids like this neighborhood.

The kids like to help the neighbors.

A neighbor asked, "Can you help dig?"

"We will help you dig!"

Kim, Pam, and Sam did it together. ▶

Close Reading Tip

Number the main events in order.

CHECK MY UNDERSTANDING

Describe the setting of the story.

_____

- -

_____

- -

_____

READ How do the kids help more neighbors?

Close Reading Tip

Put a ! by a surprising part.

A neighbor asked, "Can you see this big mess?"

"We will help you!" said the kids.

A neighbor asked, "Can you find my cat?"

"We will help you find the cat."

Then the neighbors asked, "Can you sip this?"

And the kids had many sips—happy together!

CHECK MY UNDERSTANDING

How does the story end? How do the kids feel?

_____

- -

_____

- -

_____

- -

_____

DRAW IT Draw pictures of the ways the kids help their neighbors. Then tell the story to a partner in your own words. Use your pictures to help you. Tell the main events that happen first, next, and last.

Prepare to Read

GENRE STUDY **Informational text** is nonfiction. It gives facts about a topic. Look for:

- photographs
- maps that help explain a topic
- details and facts about a topic

SET A PURPOSE Read to understand what the most important ideas are. Look for details in the words and pictures to help you. **Summarize** by telling the important ideas in your own words.

POWER WORDS

town

map

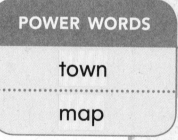

Build Background: Where We Live

On the Map!

by Lisa Fleming

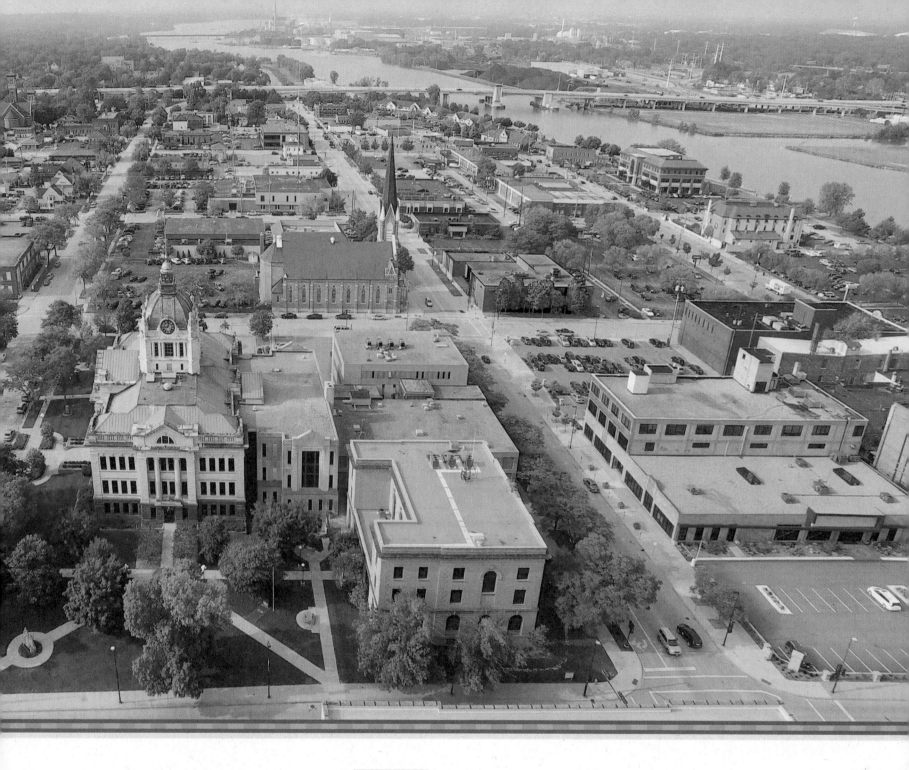

This is a town.

What do you see in the town?

Key

🏠 house
🏪 store
🏫 school
🏛 library
〜 bridge
◇ street
∿ river

This is a map of a town.
What do you see on the map?

This is a big city.
What do you see in the city?

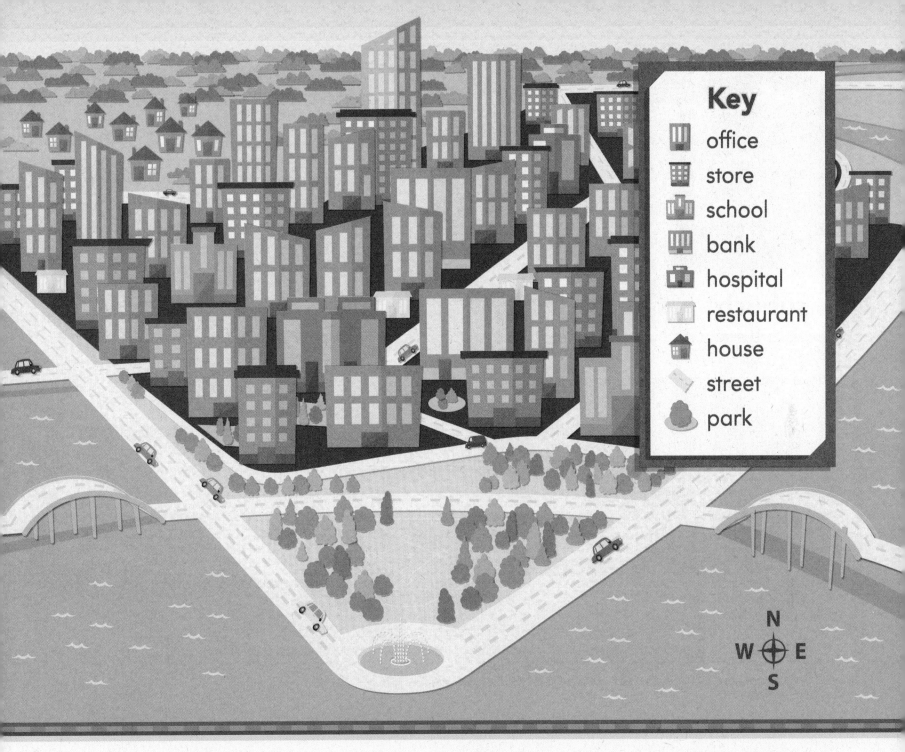

Key

office	
store	
school	
bank	
hospital	
restaurant	
house	
street	
park	

This is a map of a big city.
What do you see on the map?

suburb

farm

My Neighborhood

We live in many kinds of neighborhoods.
What is your map like?

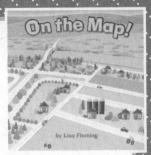

Use details from **On the Map!** to answer these questions with a partner.

1. **Summarize** What are the most important facts you learned?

2. How is a town like a city? How is it different?

💡 **Talking Tip**

Ask a question if you are not sure about your partner's ideas.

Why did you say _____?

Cite Text Evidence

READ Together

Write Directions

PROMPT Choose a map from **On the Map!** How do you get from one place to another?

PLAN First, draw or write where you start and then how to get from that place to the other place. Do you turn? What do you pass?

First

↓

Next

↓

Last

WRITE Now write directions that tell how to get from one place to another. Remember to:

- Tell each step in order.

- Use the words **first**, **next**, and **last**. Spell them correctly.

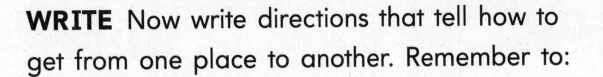

farm

Prepare to Read

GENRE STUDY **Informational text** is nonfiction. It gives facts about a topic.

MAKE A PREDICTION Preview **Neighborhoods**. Look at the text features, like the map, labels, symbols, and bold text. What do you think you will learn?

_____

- -

_____

_____

- -

_____

_____

- -

_____

SET A PURPOSE Read to find out about neighborhoods in different places.

Key
- ▬ street
- 🏠 house
- 🏢 office
- 🏫 school

Neighborhoods

READ <u>Underline</u> words the author wants you to notice.

What is a **city** like?

A city is big!

It has many **neighborhoods**.

You can see many neighbors.

You can go on a bus to a school,

a library, and a market. ▶

Close Reading Tip

Mark important ideas with *.

CHECK MY UNDERSTANDING

What important ideas did you learn from the map and text?

_____

- -

_____

- -

_____

READ What is this part mostly about?

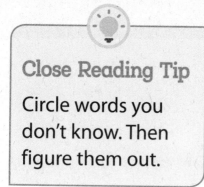

Close Reading Tip

Circle words you
don't know. Then
figure them out.

What is a **farm** like?
A farm is not as big as a city.
It is outside the city.
You do not see many neighbors.
You can go on a bus to school,
just like in a city.
Is your neighborhood like a farm?
Is it like a city?

CHECK MY UNDERSTANDING

How is the city different from the farm neighborhood?

_____

- -

_____

- -

_____

- -

_____

WRITE ABOUT IT What would it be like to live in a city or on a farm? Choose one to write about. Tell what the place is like. Use ideas from the text and pictures in **Neighborhoods**.

_____

_____

_____

_____

_____

_____

_____

_____

Prepare to Read

GENRE STUDY **Informational text** is nonfiction. It gives facts about a topic. Look for:

- facts about the world
- photos of real people and places
- headings that tell what each part is about

SET A PURPOSE **As you read, make connections** by finding ways that this text is like things in your life and other texts you have read. This will help you understand and remember the text.

POWER WORDS

community

places

purpose

clinic

Places
in My Neighborhood

by Shelly Lyons

What Is a Neighborhood?

A neighborhood is a community filled with different places to see. Each place has a special purpose that meets our needs.

Places to Live

Mia's home is in the city.

Her apartment is in a building
with many other apartments.

Jack lives in a house

in a small town.

His street is lined with homes.

Places to Keep Us Safe

Carlos visits the fire station

in his neighborhood.

The firefighters rush

to put out a fire.

Devon visits the police station.

The officer tells him

not to talk to strangers.

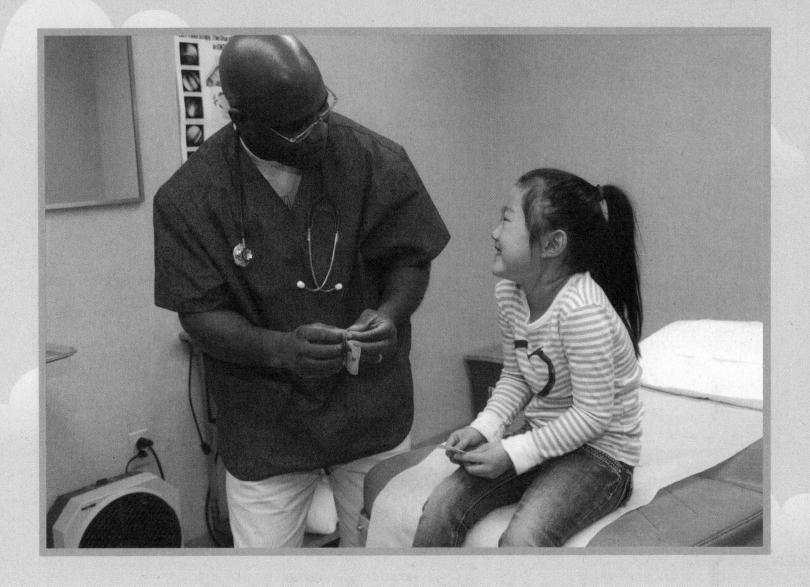

At the clinic,

a nurse gives Lila a shot.

She feels better when

she gets a bandage.

Places to Find Things

Justin bikes to the library

in his neighborhood.

He checks out books

about dinosaurs.

Jen wants fruit and milk.

At the grocery store

her dad finds fresh grapefruit.

Neighborhoods can be
big or small.
What places do you see
in your neighborhood?

Turn and Talk

Use details from **Places in My Neighborhood** to answer these questions with a partner.

1. **Make Connections** How are the neighborhoods in this text like the neighborhoods in **On the Map**?

2. How do neighborhood workers help people?

Talking Tip

Say your ideas. Be loud enough so that your partner can hear you.

I think that _____.

Write a Description

PROMPT Choose a place from **Places in My Neighborhood**. What is this place like? Use the photos and sentences for ideas.

PLAN First, write words to describe the place. Tell what you can see and hear there.

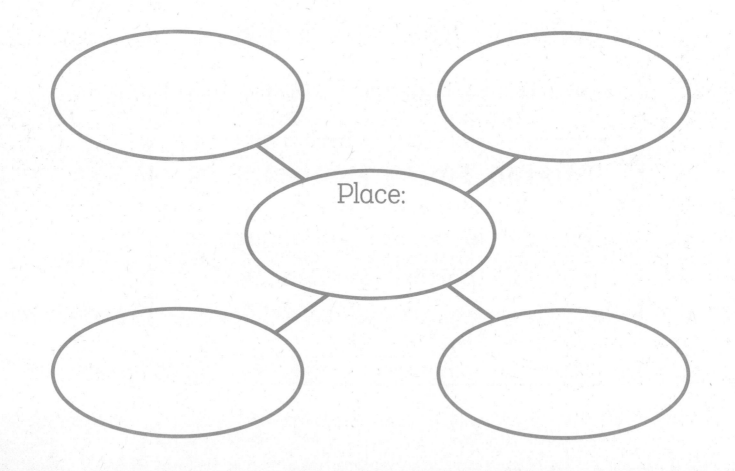

Place:

WRITE Now write sentences to describe what this place is like. Remember to:

- Use describing words.

- Add details from the photos and sentences.

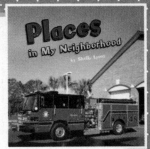

Prepare to Read

GENRE STUDY **Informational text** is nonfiction.
It gives facts about a topic.

MAKE A PREDICTION Preview **What Is This Place?**
It has riddles about places in a community.
What places do you think it will be about?

_____

- -

_____

_____

- -

_____

_____

- -

_____

SET A PURPOSE Read the clues to figure out the
riddles about places in a community. Find out
if your prediction is right.

What Is This Place?

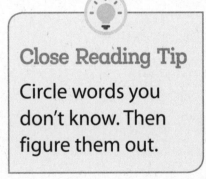

READ What are some places in a community? <u>Underline</u> them.

This place is in a community.
Neighbors find books at this place.

What is it?   A library!

You can go to this place on a bus.
Classmates go to this place.

What is it?   A school! ▶

> **Close Reading Tip**
>
> Circle words you don't know. Then figure them out.

CHECK MY UNDERSTANDING

Which words help you understand what a **library** is?

_____

- -

_____

- -

_____

This place has signs.

You go to this place with money.

You go to this place to buy and sell.

What is it? A market!

Your mom and dad go with you.

A nurse helps you in this place.

What is it? A clinic!

Close Reading Tip

Write C when you make a connection.

CHECK MY UNDERSTANDING

Which words and picture details help you understand what a **market** is?

_____

- - - - - - - - - - - - - - - - - - -

_____

_____

- - - - - - - - - - - - - - - - - - -

_____

_____

- - - - - - - - - - - - - - - - - - -

_____

WRITE ABOUT IT Think about the pictures and information in **Places in My Neighborhood** and **What Is This Place?** Write about ways that the texts are alike. Then write how they are different.

_____

- -

_____

_____

- -

_____

_____

- -

_____

_____

- -

_____

_____

- -

_____

_____

- -

_____

Prepare to Read

GENRE STUDY **Informational text** is nonfiction. It gives facts about a topic. Look for:

- facts about the world
- ways pictures and words give you information about the topic

SET A PURPOSE **Ask questions** before, during, and after you read to help you understand the text and get information. Look for evidence in the text and pictures to **answer** your questions.

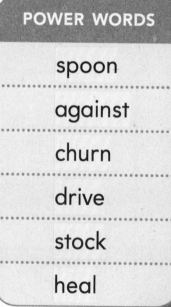

POWER WORDS

spoon

against

churn

drive

stock

heal

Meet Julie Paschkis.

WHO PUT THE COOKIES IN THE COOKIE JAR?

by **George Shannon**

illustrated by **Julie Paschkis**

One hand
in the cookie jar
takes a cookie out.

How many hands put the cookie **in**

is what the world's about.

Hands that mix and stir the dough.

Spoon the clumps into a row.

Hands that make the cookie sheet.

Oven mitts against the heat.

Hands that feed

and milk the cow.

Churn the butter.

Guide the plow.

Hands that sow
and grind the wheat

into flour for us to eat.

Hands that tend and feed the hens.

Gather eggs. Build the pens.

Hands that harvest sugarcane.
Cut and grind.
Load the train.

Hands that load the trucks and drive.

164

Stock the shelves when things arrive.

Hands that clothe and feed them all.
Heal and teach.
Large and small.

Hands that help
the hands that help
are what the world's about . . .

. . . **many** put
the cookie in,

so **one** can
take it out.

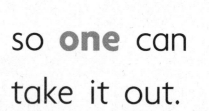

SUGAR COOKIES

1 cup sugar
½ cup unsalted butter, melted
1 egg
2 tablespoons milk
2 teaspoons vanilla
1 ½ cups all-purpose flour
½ teaspoon baking powder
½ teaspoon salt

- Preheat oven to 375 degrees.

- Grease 2 cookie sheets.

- Combine sugar, melted butter, egg, milk, and vanilla. Beat or stir until smooth.

- In a small bowl, combine flour, baking powder, and salt.

- Add the flour mixture to the sugar mixture and beat or stir until combined.

- Drop teaspoons of dough onto a cookie sheet, and press each cookie down with the bottom of a glass or the palm of your hand.

- Bake 10 to 12 minutes at 375 degrees, until the edges just begin to turn golden brown. Cool for 2 minutes on the cookie sheets, then transfer to cooling racks.

Makes about 3 dozen cookies.

READ
Together

Turn and Talk

Use details from **Who Put the Cookies in the Cookie Jar?** to answer these questions with a partner.

1. **Ask and Answer Questions** What questions did you have before, during, and after reading the text? How did the questions help you understand the information?

2. What jobs do people do to help make cookies?

Talking Tip

Use this sentence to add your own idea to what your partner says.

My idea is _____.

Write a Thank-You Note

PROMPT Choose a worker to thank from **Who Put the Cookies in the Cookie Jar?** Why do you think the person is helpful?

PLAN First, draw a picture of the person. Show what they do to help make the cookies.

WRITE Now write a note to thank the person. Tell why what they do helps make the cookies. Remember to:

- Write the word **I** with a capital letter.

- Sign your name. Begin it with a capital letter.

Prepare to Read

GENRE STUDY **Informational text** is nonfiction. It gives facts about a topic.

MAKE A PREDICTION Preview **Kids Can Help**. It tells how kids can help make cookies. What do you think you will learn about?

_____

_____

_____

_____

SET A PURPOSE Ask yourself questions before, during, and after you read to help yourself understand the different jobs kids can do to help.

Kids Can Help

READ <u>Underline</u> the jobs kids can do to help make cookies.

Who wants to help make cookies?

Kids can do many jobs to help.

Kids can get the spoons and pans.

Kids can mix with the spoons.

Kids can not do one job.

Mom will put the pan in. ▶

Close Reading Tip

Put a **?** by the parts you have questions about.

CHECK MY UNDERSTANDING

Describe one of the jobs kids can do.

_____

_____

_____

_____

175

READ <u>Underline</u> the jobs kids can do to help clean up.

Can kids help with the mess?

Yes! Kids can get the mop and mop up the room.

Kids can find the spoons.

But kids can not take the hot cookies out.

Dad will do this job.

Kids can do one last job.

Kids can enjoy the cookies! Yum!

CHECK MY UNDERSTANDING

Write a question you still have about **Kids Can Help**.

_____

- -

_____

_____

- -

_____

_____

- -

_____

WRITE ABOUT IT The author describes different jobs in **Kids Can Help**. What are some jobs kids can do? Why is describing one job after another a good way for the author to give the information?

_____

- -

_____

- -

_____

_____

- -

_____

_____

- -

_____

- -

_____

- -

_____

- -

_____

Prepare to View

GENRE STUDY **Videos** are short movies. Some videos give information. Others are for you to watch for enjoyment. Watch and listen for:

- the purpose of the video
- information about the topic
- the language and the words used

SET A PURPOSE Find out about jobs. Listen for new words about jobs. Use clues in the sentences you hear and the pictures to help you understand the meanings of the words.

Build Background: Interesting Jobs

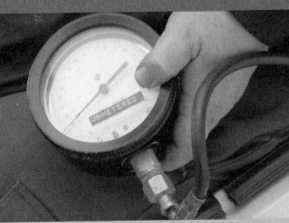

Curious About Jobs

As You View Listen for special words like **mechanic**, **potter**, and **museum**. They tell about certain jobs. Use the sentences the children say and the pictures to help you understand what these special words mean.

Turn and Talk

Curious About Jobs

Use details from **Curious About Jobs** to answer these questions with a partner.

1. **Content-Area Words** How does each worker do his or her job? Use some new words you learned to help you explain.

2. Which job is most interesting to you? Use details from the video to tell why.

Talking Tip

Say your ideas. Speak clearly and not too fast or too slow.

I think that _____.

Let's Wrap Up!

? Essential Question

How does everyone in my family and community make them special?

Pick one of these activities to show what you have learned about the topic.

1. Act It Out

Choose one of the community places you have read about. Work with a partner. Act out things you can do in that place. Can your other classmates guess the place?

2. Award Time

You have read about special people in families and in the community. Who deserves an award? Make the award. Then write sentences. Tell why the person deserves it.

My Notes

Glossary

A

against   If one thing is used against another, it keeps something from being harmed. Wear a coat to stay warm **against** the cold.

area   An area is a part of a bigger place. My class has a special **area** to play in at school.

B

beautiful   Something that is beautiful is nice to look at. The flowers are **beautiful** colors.

C

challenge   A challenge is something that is hard to do. Running up a big hill is a **challenge**.

changed   If something changed, it became different from what it was. The caterpillar **changed** into a butterfly!

chilly   When something is chilly, it is cold. Put on a coat if you are **chilly**.

churn   When you churn something, you stir it quickly for a long time. **Churn** the cream until it turns into butter.

clinic   A clinic is a place where people go to see a doctor or nurse. Did you go to a **clinic** when you cut your foot?

community A community is made up of people who live near each other and the places around them. We all went to see the parade in our **community**.

D

drive When you drive something, you make it go where you want it to go. The racers **drive** their cars around the track.

E

emotions Emotions are strong feelings we have, like happiness or sadness. We feel happy **emotions** when our team wins.

enjoy If you enjoy doing something, you really like it. We **enjoy** watching movies.

excited When you feel excited, you are very happy. The **excited** children cheered when they got their prizes.

F

friendship When you have a friendship with someone, you like the person. Our nice **friendship** started the day we met.

G

great Something that is great is better than good. We love to eat the **great** food Mom makes.

H

heal When doctors heal sick or hurt people, they help them get well. She put a bandage on my hand to **heal** it.

help When you help, you make it easier for someone to do something. I **help** my dad do the dishes.

K

kinds If there are many kinds of something, there are many different groups of it. We saw all **kinds** of animals at the zoo.

L

last When something happens at last, it happens after a long time. We waited, and the school bus came at **last**.

M

map A map is a picture that shows streets, rivers, and other parts of a place. I can find many places on the **map**.

market A market is a place where people can buy things. We go to the **market** to buy food.

mess If something is a mess, it is not neat. I cleaned up the **mess** in my room.

N

neighbors Your neighbors are the people who live near you. We talk to the **neighbors** we see next door.

nervous When you feel nervous, you are worried about what might happen. I was **nervous** the first time I tried to ride a bike.

new When something is new, you have never seen, had, or done it before. I am going to a **new** school this year.

P

paddled If you paddled through water, you swam by moving your hands and feet. He jumped in the pool and **paddled** to the side.

partner A partner is someone you work with or play with. My **partner** and I make something together.

places Places are certain parts of a city or town. Does your town have **places** to ride bikes?

population The population is the number of people who live in a place. The crowded city has a big **population**.

purpose A purpose is a reason for doing or having something. The **purpose** of the sign is to tell drivers to stop.

S

sell When you sell something, you give it to someone who gives you money for it. I get some money when I **sell** things.

set When you set something up, you make it so that it is useful. Let's **set** up tables for the party.

spoon When you spoon food, you pick it up with a spoon. **Spoon** the food into the baby's mouth.

stock When you stock something, you fill it up with things. **Stock** the empty shelf with cans of food.

T

together When friends do things together, they do them with each other. The friends play a game **together**.

town A town is a place where people live that is smaller than a city. We know most of the people in our small **town**.

trip When you go on a trip, you go from one place to another. My family took a **trip** to the lake.

try When you try to do something, you work at doing it. Every day, I **try** to learn to ride my bike.

U

ugly   If something is ugly, it is not nice to look at. I like green, but my friend thinks it is **ugly**.

W

wished   If you wished for something, you wanted it to happen. I **wished** for a new game for my birthday.

working   If you are working, you are doing a job. They are **working** to build a car.

Index of Titles and Authors

Acknowledgments

Excerpt from *First Girl Scout* by Ginger Wadsworth. Text copyright © 2012 by Clarion Books, an imprint of Houghton Mifflin Harcourt. Reprinted by permission of Houghton Mifflin Harcourt Publishing Company.

Places in My Neighborhood by Shelly Lyons. Text copyright © 2013 by Capstone Press, a Capstone imprint. Reprinted by permission of Capstone Press Publishers.

Who Put the Cookies in the Cookie Jar? by George Shannon, illustrated by Julie Paschkis. Text copyright © 2013 by George Shannon. Illustrations copyright © 2013 by Julie Paschkis. Reprinted by arrangement with Henry Holt Books for Young Readers, and by permission of Sheldon Fogelman and Wernick & Pratt Agency.

Credits

4 (c) ©Houghton Mifflin Harcourt; 4 (c) ©suzieleakey/iStock/Getty Images, (bg) ©ayelet-keshet/Shutterstock; 5 (t) ©Lise Gagne/E+/Getty Images; 5 (t) ©The FuZees; 5 (bg) ©The FuZees; 5 (bg) ©The FuZees; 5 (bg) ©Lise Gagne/E+/Getty Images, (cr) ©WhitePlaid/Shutterstock, (bl) ©GlobalStock/Vetta/Getty Images, (tr) ©paulaphoto/Shutterstock; 6 (cl) ©BJI/Blue Jean Images/Getty Images, (bcl) ©Scholastic Studio 10/Photolibrary/Getty Images, (c) ©Kalmatsuy/ Shutterstock, (cr) ©drbimages/iStock/Getty Images Plus/ Getty Images; 7 (t) ©Tom Fawls/Dreamstime; 7 (bl) (all) ©Clarion Books/Houghton Mifflin Company; 8 (br) ©sutham/Shutterstock, (bl) ©kaloriya/Fotolia, (bg) ©Dan Sedran/Shutterstock, (bcl) ©m-imagephotography/iStock/Getty Images Plus/Getty Images; 12 (c) ©suzieleakey/iStock/Getty Images, (bg) ©ayelet-keshet/Shutterstock; 14 ©Sean Masterson; 15 ©Houghton Mifflin Harcourt; 16 (tl) ©GS/Gallery Stock Limited; 16 (tr) ©Aaron Belford/Dreamstime; 16 (bl) ©JGI/Jamie Grill/ Media Bakery; 16 (br) ©Monkey Business Images/ Dreamstime; 17 ©Houghton Mifflin Harcourt; 18 ©Houghton Mifflin Harcourt; 19 ©Houghton Mifflin Harcourt; 20 ©GS/Gallery Stock Limited; 21 ©Houghton Mifflin Harcourt; 22 ©FatCamera/ iStock/Getty Images; 23 ©Houghton Mifflin Harcourt; 24 (tl) ©Houghton Mifflin Harcourt; 24 (tr) ©FatCamera/iStock/Getty Images Plus/Getty Images; 24 (bl) ©asiseeit/iStock/Getty Images Plus/ Getty Images; 24 (br) ©Houghton Mifflin Harcourt; 25 (tr) ©Houghton Mifflin Harcourt; 27 (tr) ©Houghton Mifflin Harcourt; 32 ©Elisa Chavarri; 50 ©PeopleImages/iStock/Getty Images Plus/Getty Images; 51 (c) ©Lise Gagne/E+/Getty Images, (cr) ©WhitePlaid/Shutterstock, (bl) ©GlobalStock/Vetta/Getty Images, (tr) ©paulaphoto/Shutterstock; 52 ©kali9/E+/Getty Images; 53 (tl) ©Pressmaster/Shutterstock; 53 (tr) ©Huntstock/Getty Images; 53 (cl) ©Amble Design/ Shutterstock; 53 (cr) ©Hero Images/Digital Vision/ Getty Images; 53 (bl) ©Monkey Business Images/ Shutterstock; 53 (br) ©WhitePlaid/Shutterstock; 54 ©dbimages/Alamy; 55 (tl) ©GlobalStock/Vetta/ Getty Images; 55 (tr) ©Hero Images/Alamy; 55 (cl) ©Pressmaster/Shutterstock; 55 (cr) ©MBI/Alamy; 55 (bl) ©Hero Images/Getty Images; 55 (br) ©Jurgen Magg/Alamy; 56 ©Monkey Business Images/Shutterstock; 57 ©Alinute Silzeviciute/ Shutterstock; 58 ©szefei/iStock/Getty Images Plus/ Getty Images; 59 (tl) ©Amble Design/Shutterstock; 59 (tr) ©kali9/E+/Getty Images; 59 (cl) ©Image Source Trading Ltd/Shutterstock; 59 (cr) ©implementarfilms/Fotolia; 59 (bl) ©MN Studio/ Shutterstock; 59 (br) ©Media Photos/iStock/Getty Images Plus/Getty Images; 60 ©paulaphoto/ Shutterstock; 61 (c) ©Lise Gagne/E+/Getty Images, (cr) ©WhitePlaid/Shutterstock, (bl) ©GlobalStock/ Vetta/Getty Images, (tr) ©paulaphoto/Shutterstock; 63 (c) ©Lise Gagne/E+/Getty Images, (cr) ©WhitePlaid/Shutterstock, (bl) ©GlobalStock/Vetta/ Getty Images, (tr) ©paulaphoto/Shutterstock; 68 ©Gail Carson Levine; 86 ©The FuZees; 87 (all) ©The FuZees; 88 ©The FuZees; 89 (tr) ©The FuZees; 89 (tr) ©The FuZees; 89 (tr) ©The FuZees; 90 ©OlScher/Shutterstock; 91 (r) ©yasinguneysu/ iStockPhoto.com; 91 (l) ©Rawpixel.com/ Shutterstock; 96 (br) ©snake3d/iStock/Getty Images Plus/Getty Images; 97 (l) ©Kalmatsuy/ Shutterstock; 97 (r) ©drbimages/iStock/Getty Images Plus/Getty Images; 98 ©Wong Herbert Yee; 120 ©dibrova/Shutterstock; 122 ©JamesBrey/ istock/Getty Images Plus/Getty Images; 124 ©6381380/iStock/Getty Images Plus/Getty Images; 126 (t) ©Craig Tuttle/Design Pics/Getty Images; 126 (b) ©Filtv/Dreamstime; 126 (r) ©Kleber Cordeiro costa/Alamy; 134 (bg) ©Tom Fawls/ Dreamstime; 134 (br) ©imantsu/iStock/Getty Images Plus/Getty Images; 136 ©JayLazarin/ iStock/Getty Images; 137 ©trekandshoot/ Shutterstock; 138 ©DNY59/E+/Getty Images; 139 ©Capstone Studio/Karon Dubke; 140 ©Capstone Studio/Karon Dubke; 141 ©Capstone Studio/Karon Dubke; 142 ©phi2/iStock/Getty Images Plus/Getty Images; 143 ©Capstone Studio/Karon Dubke; 144 ©Capstone Studio/Karon Dubke; 145 (tr) ©Tom Fawls/Dreamstime; 147 (tr) ©Tom Fawls/ Dreamstime; 148 (l) ©SelectStock/iStock/Getty Images Plus; 148 (r) ©Ceri Breeze/Shutterstock; 148 (t) ©umiberry/Shutterstock; 149 (l) ©Tyler Olson/Shutterstock; 149 (r) ©Monkey Business Images/Shutterstock; 150 ©Ceri Breeze/ Shutterstock; 152 ©Joe Max Emminger; 178 ©inhauscreative/iStock/Getty Images Plus/Getty Images; 179 ©Clarion Books/Houghton Mifflin Company; 179 (all) ©Clarion Books/Houghton Mifflin Company; 180 ©Clarion Books/Houghton Mifflin Company; 181 (all) ©Clarion Books/ Houghton Mifflin Company; 182 ©Apple's Eyes Studio/Shutterstock; 183 ©Igor Kisselev/Getty Images